Thank you so much f

gave to me in past few monins. i m very .....,

book as it is my first time when my poem got published and I want thought to show my gratitude to you through this mail. Hope we get to work together again in the future and wishing you all the best for future endeavours.- Mitali Prasad

I am already a follower of your Instagram and Facebook page, since December 2020 and find the contents thoroughly enjoyable.- Swarnadip Chatterjee

Hi there, I just wanted to say that after reading some of the poetry on Wingless Dreamer, I feel inspired and in awe. I've been writing on and off as a hobby for a few years now but seeing what you've done and how you've built this whole community of writers, I'm really inspired and impressed. You've given me just a bit more inspiration to keep working on my projects and for that I thank you.- Ryan

Best of afternoons! I am Arnaldo Batista, author of the poem "Hypochondriac Thriving," that your publication has chosen to enter in your "Fruits of our Quarantine" contest. I am simply sending this email to first thank you for this as I am truly humbled by your decision to accept this poem for publication. I wrote this poem after many nights of night terrors and panic attacks due to my looming anxiety over the pandemic and instant changes the world is going through seemingly overnight. Your validation of this poem is received by such validation and a feeling of triumph that I cannot put into words, so genuinely, thank you. -Arnaldo Batista

Proud and grateful to be included in one of your previous books. I will purchase and help promote your continued good work- J Brooke

It took me so long to get into reading & writing poetry, but last summer, I finally felt inspired to do it. In December 2019, I was published for the first time as a poet!! My poem is featured in the winter edition of Passionate Penholders by @winglessdreamer1 (available on Amazon) Poetry is always so relaxing to me and I hope that during this time of "unknowns," hopefully, we can all be inspired to relax a little and curl up with some good poetry! It's finally here!!! I am officially a published author check it out for yourself on Amazon! Thank you @winglessdreamer1 for believing in my work! – Landri Driskill

Keep up this excellent work. Poetry truly connects the readers with poetic souls across countries and cultures – Amita Sanghvi

It is a great joy for me that a kindhearted editor of a journal like you has liked my poem. Thank you again. I am hundred percent willing to publish my poem, "Oh beautiful beloved" in The book issue called Diversity: There's a beauty in that too. I am pasting my updated bio below. Be happy in life this is my heartfelt wishes to you.-Sandip Saha

I truly admire their creative publication who works so hard to promote emerging writers and artists for what they truly deserve and make them feel much appreciated. Hats off.-Josh Sullivan

Unlike traditional publisher Wingless Dreamer has supported and encouraged me to a great extent. -Sowmyata Singh

Wingless Dreamer

CULTURAL REGENERATION THROUGH OUR CREATIVE COMMUNITY

HEARTFELT POETRY COLLECTION

Edited by

RUCHI ACHARYA

ABOUT US

The Wingless Dreamer Community was founded by Ruchi Acharya to bridge the gap between emerging writers or artists and traditional publishing. Ruchi's community is a global platform for those who truly believe in themselves and are passionate about writing or illustrating. It's the dream of her community to create a space where the authors or artists are free to express themselves.

Wingless Dreamer slowly but steadily grew with artists and writers from all over the world. Over time Wingless Dreamer became the main stage for well-known professional writers and artists to express themselves, all at the same place.

We envisioned a community where writers and artists would be invited to publish solely based on the merit of their writing and creative skills. The Wingless Dreamer community connects all essences of writing, illustrating, editing, marketing, and promoting on a single platform so that authors and illustrators don't have to go through the hardships of the publishing processes and focus on their work. The Community members become part of the family and are guided, supported, and encouraged on every step they make towards their writing and art career. The members can get access to free critiques, reviews, marketing, and in some cases funding for their work via email.

Our Wingless Dreamer team spends lots of time and energy to create as many contests as possible on different themes every quarter so that writers and artists can truly enjoy their experience with us.
The community is still growing and its accomplished authors and artists speak for themselves.

"Being a writer can sometimes be solitary and quiet. A writer can understand how it feels to fall in love with every single character, to battle with dialogues, to work with vivid poetic devices, to endeavor for perfection and to build an entire universe from scratch. Guess what? You're not alone. We understand the efforts you put every day into your work. Since we are a team of writers and artists too.

The art and writing industry is always considered as something obscure and profound by the public in general. It has become so difficult to stand alone and be noticed in the art industry or to stick with a writing career in the commercial society we live in today. Compared to other financial and economic-related jobs, things related to art are the minority.

Art and poetry are the most important elements of our life as it helps us understand and appreciate the world around us. No matter what anybody tells you words and ideas have the power to change the world and sneaks the truth upon you.

One of my favorite quotes:

We don't read and write poetry because it's cute. We read and write poetry because we are members of the human race. And the human race is filled with passion. And medicine, law, business, engineering, these are noble pursuits and necessary to sustain life. But poetry, beauty, romance, love, these are what we stay alive for.-N.H. Kleinbaum, Dead Poets Society

In the end I would like to urge all the people who are reading this to never ever give up on your dreams. Seize the day. Every day counts. You're art. Never step back from showing your creative side to the world. It's beautiful."

-Ruchi Acharya, Wingless Dreamer Founder

R.Acharya

-Ruchi Acharya

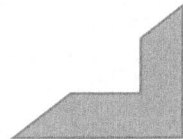

CONTENTS

Believe in yourself

I want to use this opportunity to thank all the participants, Winglessdreamer's team and community members to make this publication possible. Thanks for the support and well-wishes.

–Ruchi Acharya (Wingless Dreamer Founder)

1. ANNIE KEY

Little Annie.
Don't be gun coy. Be trigger happy.
Aim right between fuel and flame.
Occupy a space on the cusp of dusk.
An oil slick to drown us all,
In the darkness of a closed mouth.

Be the baddest apple in the orchard
But stitch sweetness on your tongue.
Cut your slice then poison the pie.
Then you better run.

They think you're porcelain,
They think you're shy.
But you're a petrol rainbow
That can blow up the sky.

The little red girl in *Schindler's List.*
A colour shock that can't be missed.

Censoring you is punching confetti.
A vivacious kitty with volatility.
Nine whole lives of ambiguity.
Nine whole lives of fucking anarchy.

CHRISTIAN DEERY

Christian Deery is a 33 year old MA Writing graduate from Warwick University. He studies
a hip-hop for inspiration, and his favourite artists include Kanye West and Frank Ocean.
Other influences are the characters he encounters in his world famous hometown of Rugby.
His favourite author is Chuck Palahniuk

2. THE LEPER COLONY

Here's more than rocks and scrubby pine, this isle
Each woman wearing hoods of green and rum
Will pace the walls and whisper every mile
In pain they live, but ghosts they have become

Old Charlotte screams for fingers and for toes
No visitors, no friends, no memories
I know the signs, I feel my wounds necrose
And know that soon I'll travel to that isle

A secret, for as long as I can bear
Until it is external, I'll beware
So unprepared, to die before i'm dead
I'll drink the wine, I'll chew upon the bread
Prolong my time alive is all I wish
I'd rather be a fisherman or fish

LAURA MARSHALL

My name is Laura Marshall, and I am an aspiring writer and undergraduate English student at Brigham Young University, in Utah. I am attracted to the freedom of creative non-fiction, but have also tested my strength in both poetry and narrative fiction. In my free time, I do collage art.-Laura

3. CRISS CROSS APPLESAUCE

sitting criss cross applesauce
in the laundry basket, you'd fly
me high around the house, like
i was an astronaut in space and
i'd laugh and laugh because i
knew nothing could ever stop you.

sitting criss cross applesauce
on your bedroom floor, i'd listen
to your stories, days when you'd
count coins for coke bottles and
i'd laugh and laugh because i
knew nothing could ever stop you.

sitting criss cross applesauce
in the stillness of your house, i listen
as you call me by my mother's name,
and i smile politely, remembering
how we once laughed and laughed
and nothing could ever stop you.

sitting criss cross applesauce
in my makeshift apartment in your
old spare room, tears stream down
my cheeks as i remember the days
we used to laugh and laugh, when
i thought nothing could ever stop you

AMANDA HELD

Amanda Held is a midwest native poet. She earned her Bachelor of Arts in writing from Carroll University in 2014. Some of Amanda's previously published work has appeared in Century Magazine, Indolent Books, and Awakenings. In her free time, Amand enjoys spending time in the outdoors, board gaming, and playing with her tiny cat son.

4. QUEENS OF THE FOREST

The graceful oak
overshadows the humble dandelion
while a sneaky little vine winds around its
scarred trunk and swaying branches.
A seemingly permanent aspect of the forest
yet it dies a tiny fraction of a molecule with every
passing minute.
The previous behemoths now lay as tumbled rotting heaps
of twisted limbs and moss covered logs,
reminding the living that they will not remain for long.
Every winter's temporary death
is one season closer to the final swaying
of a majestic Queen of the forest
as she begins her devastating plunge,
taking all who stand in her path with her,
demonstrating her power even in her final moments
of life.

LAURA AUSTIN

Laura has been previously published in Better Than Starbucks Magazine, Czykmate Productions, Poet's Choice, and The Haberdasher. She proudly serves as a judge for Ageless Authors and has self-published two children's books.

5. OBLIVION

The blessing of forgetting is life seems anew
The curse of forgetting is life is never whole
You can build a nation, a culture on a dream
But to dream you need the sleep of oblivion
So the prickly memories can run away
Split and hide in unlooked crevices
Allowing the birth of a new order
on collective amnesia.
But the past is never lost to the future
The unvisited corners demand their day
They carry around pangs of separation
Disregarded, unacknowledged, unowned
Lingering in the abode of non-understanding
Present without cognition or language
The sleep has dismembered them
And now they seek the demise of the order
And an awakening of the whole
Unmodeled in body and mind
Unhesitant in receiving the unknown

AMIR HUDA

Dr. Amir Huda is a recently retired professor of medical physics who is dabbling in the arts these days and thoroughly loving it!

6. BLUE MOON

Dark light, Blue moon fills the heart of empty men
Sadistic women preying on the living, filled with envy
Crippled by men, she sworn to be free

The sadistic women is the blue moon, grasping all men virginity
Casting shadows, filled with crying joy, brought sorrow to the night sky
She white and an invisible, only men of heart dream to see her

A soft kiss she brings but a curse she leaves, leaving your soul darker than it
was before
Manmade whore consumed by her brilliances, forever more she will be adored
Golden tongues speak of her in the night sky, gyrate into universal space
Sexy twisted manipulated beast runs free in the forest howling at the moon

Forever blue she will be, for she is filled with wisdom beyond her years
Sacred and new to the world, for only in a blue moon she appears
Naked and free she is, craving virgin blood under a blue moon filled with lust

Going to church praying for more for this sweet nectar called sex
Blue moon, sadistic and free, men grovel after her
Under her spell you are taken, another victim she consumes
She is a woman, she is addictive
Women is what she will be called, forever she will be known

MICHAEL KING

I was born in Romania and I'm going to school to become a secondary history educator. I
enjoy musical theare, rock climbing, and finding opportunities to inspire change through
poetry. I have writing poetry and plays for years as way to connect with others. I have autism
and poetry is my doorway to connecting with others. I hope to continue to inspire faith and
love through poetry for the next generation to come. I want to bring awarness to serious
ongoing issues and continue to be a voice for those who are foced to be silent and can't speak
for themselves. These poems addresses several emotional topics being sexaul violence
toward women and suicide caused by school bullying.- Michael

7. FEBRUARY ICE IN THE SKY

The sky has become a sheet of ice,
A glacier spread above the planet.

In true winter, cold as bone-chilling
It can be. A vast and unchanging sky.

The sight is tranquil as someone passes
By while walking or driving. It knows no bounds.

The heart is lulled in waves as if trying to
Keep from falling asleep. Breathe or not to.

And yet, breathing keeps the body alive.
The mind thinks this and it is a blue radiance outside.

In February filled with a glassy sort of sky.
A tower of cloudless paste with perfection.

No cuts, no indentions. A spread of ice
Or ice cream before it gets sullied by the sun.

ANNIE TRAN

Annie Tran is the author of "The Bride Who Never Was", which is included in Issue 7 of Route 7 Review's online journal. She graduated from the University of Texas at Dallas with a BA in Literary Studies, and is continuing her education there for her MA in Literature. While concentrating on creative writing, she works as a Fiction/Translation reader for Reunion: The Dallas Review. She also dives into writing some queer works.

8. GRACE

Wiping dust and dirt, streaks of black not completely gone yet
Vacuuming bits of papers and remnants from the floor
Hearing the swoosh of the washer in the background
Boxes stacked neatly in the corner, remaining
Smelling bleach and Windex in the air
Bags of garbage, waiting by the door
Left with a bare, white, square room
Smoothing out holes with putty
I am tired but I miss you already
Mom

CAROL BAKER

Carol Baker is an undergraduate student at Arizona State University with an emphasis in Women and Gender Studies. She is a modern, stoic feminist who supports her follow writers who continue to tell the truth and live life with meaning.

9. WORDS AND PHRASES

If words your beauty could define I'd write
A thousand lines to those alluring eyes,
A hundred cantos dedicated to
The face and hue my ecstasy induced;
A hundred thousand stanzas I'd create,
A thousand thousand petty phrases shaped
With unembellished praises of the smile
When parted my unworthy heart beguiles.

But nothing versed or penned could yet aspire
To recreate in words and sounds the fire
Your peerless visage kindles in my soul,
And never wrote a poet, young or old,
Adept enough with language to construct
A proper written copy of my love.

JAMES HUSS

James Lewis Huss is the quintessential scholar warrior. An award-winning poet, playwright, and novelist, he is also a highly skilled martial artist and teacher who travels the world sharing his knowledge of both the arts of war and of letters. James has a BA in English with a concentration in writing from University of South Carolina and an MA in English from Northwestern State University of Louisiana. James currently teaches English language and literature in Taiwan.

10. SOUTHERN CALIFORNIA SUMMERS

(Submitted by Erin chalk on behalf of visually impaired student Kylie Sykes)

Imagine the heat
BEATING down on you!
With some wild, whipping
wind — added in.

Imagine the soothing sounds
of classic music playing
a soundtrack while doing yard work,
or simply sitting around.

Imagine tons of vacations
(camping, flying, and cruising, too).
After all, it's summertime relaxation
Which needs no explanation!

KYLIE SYKES

Kylie Sykes absolutely enjoys all art disciplines including painting, drawing, mosaic, photography, and more. In addition, she has had the opportunity to submit her poetry to contests throughout Los Angeles and Orange counties, and she loves the experience of writing poems to share with others.

11. ANYONE BUT YOU

It should have been
anyone but you
asking me how many
men there have been.

Anyone but you
who would think the answer
should be none.

Anyone but you
who would judge me based
on who had touched me
years ago.

Anyone but you
who would think my value lay
in purity and chastity.

Anyone but you
who couldn't see me
as more than that.

JODIE BAEYENS

Jodie Baeyens is a professor at American Military University. She was deposited in Arizona from Manhattan, against her will, and now lives in a rural farming community writing poetry and drinking red wine.

12. MOONLIT

This instrument that I adore—
It looks like you, in colors true;
Ivory keys like moonlight beams
And pitch black notes adorned with red

The moonlit keys are like your face,
The jet black keys are like your hair,
And red felt strips across them both
Are like your lips that pulse with love

This instrument I do adore—
Its deep, pure tones console my heart
But you—there's nothing that can ever match—
You Angel from the moonlit night

TANIA PRZYWARA

Tania Przywara is a lover of all things beautiful, including music, nature, photography, and poetry. First and foremost a musician, her artistic passions often intertwine, resulting in a unique creative fusion of music, poetry, and visuals. Tania is very honored to be able to share her poetry inspired by love, as love to her is the most beautiful thing of all.

13. I USED TO PRAY BEFORE PLANE RIDES

It has already happened
Because by the time you notice

Like scars fading
Or your nails growing

Pandemics unfathomable
Decades unthinkable

Treasures untouched by travesties
Minutes seemed longer back then

I used to pray before plane rides

I used to get excited about pancakes

Like post-dusk cement on bare feet
Like the smell of lavender,
I long for the simpler nights

When did clouds become clouds with silver linings?

Driving us insane
It's all the same isolation

The thought of sleep feels frightening

Vulnerability playing conquer and divide

Anxiety setting in
from a nightmare last night

I see the carcass of my brother

THERESE POKORNEY

Therese is an unpublished poet from Chicago; however, she currently resides in Astoria, Oregon where she works remotely and surfs in her free time. She just graduated from the University of Illinois at Urbana-Champaign where she studied journalism and psychology.

14. HOT GIRL AT DRUG COURT

Your eyes, for a moment, met with mine...
But you were looking at seven years jail time.
OoOoO you're a bad girl, huh?
Fiery haired wicked angel.
Sweet Shiva — Goddess of self-destruction.
Love skeletons in your bedroom's closet.
Junk withdrawal — Suffering — Sadness.
Let me be the spike in your vein,
That takes all your pain away.

GREG WILDER

Greg Wilder (also known by the stage name Slay! the Dragon) is an award-winning writer, full-time student, and spoken word performer, currently residing in Schenectady, N.Y. After a long, downhill battle with alcohol and drug addiction, Greg entered treatment in June of 2017 and rediscovered the therapeutic potential of art and writing. Today, with over 3 years clean, Greg shares the healing power of poetry with other recovering addicts as an intern for a drug and alcohol treatment center. Greg received an A.A.S. in Human Services from SUNY Schenectady in May of 2020.

15. STILLED WAKEFULNESS

light fades from
an operatic day's sky
and silence then begins to stir
the storm
of nocturnal notes,
unsleeping night's eyes;

where insomniacs will die
a thousand deaths

* before they die *

SARAHA O' LEARY

A Profoundly Deaf Poet. A Dreamer. A Believer. A Lover of Words/Paper and how they feel. With no formal training in writing and a self confessed poor student, SarahA O'Leary credits her ability to write Poems through being denied one of the Poets principle muses - her hearing. When something is taken away, it is always replaced by something far greater.

16. GASP

There's a moment just before
ink dries, before thought solidifies,
before paper sucks the essence of its composer-
the space between death and dying-

where I dare to live.

ALCION THOMAS

My name is Alcion Thomas and I have recently graduated from the University of North Florida, with a major in English and a minor in Business. In my spare time, I appreciate impromptu picnics and watching slam poetry. When not spending time outdoors or lost in literature, I maintain two online stores, encourage children to read, and blog about local businesses. Writing has served as an outlet for my emotions and as a coping mechanism for life's most unexpected moments. I am truly grateful for the selection of my poem 'pillow talk', written at one of my most indecisive hours. Amidst my doubt and self-loathe, 'pillow talk' became the poem to embody my unstable stream of consciousness at that moment.

17. PSYCHEDELIC

I am ending in a bokeh
of fairy lights, a hue cycle of chroma
varnished with colors I've never seen.

I am ending in shades
of tinted undertones,
each daub – a mistaken grief,
a frescoed canvas of forgotten friends.

I am ending in vibgyor verses
of laminated whitewash,
taken aback by the splendor
of a graying, black and white.

I am ending in a rainbow, a spectrum of saturation.
Withal and although, my prismatic cessation.

PRIYA TAMANG

Priya Dolma Tamang is a medical graduate from the north-east Indian state of Sikkim. With her tribal Nepali roots and deeply seated Buddhist beliefs, culture and mindfulness have both been active themes in her writing.

18. BLOOM

What can you do when the world is in bloom
And you cannot feel it in your heart?
Do you cry?
Do you laugh?
Do you let yourself go mad?
Or do you just try to hold fast
Knowing the season will come again
And perhaps that next time,
You can bloom with it.

JONATHAN HUGHES

I'm a Florida native born in 1991. Growing up I lived an average, normal life in many ways, but it wasn't without its fair share problems from police calls and custody changes. In 2011 it came to a head with the passing of my father and again with the passing of my mother in 2017. Hoping to find solace and forge a new path, I moved to California in 2018. I'm not sure if this is my true home, but I love the landscape. Much of my inspiration comes from nature and it can easily be found in my poetry. I feel plain observation holds the answers to questions about life and existence.- Jonathan

19. ONCE UPON A VALENTINE- A VILLIANELLE

Once upon a Valentine when they met,
An evening when soft were sun's rays
When his heart for sorrow was not set.

A virgin love that does not end at bed,
A love which is rare, rare to find these days;
Once upon a Valentine when they met.

When women by men, on sheets, were bled;
He toiled to create for her a word maze,
When his heart for sorrow was not set.

It was his dreams on which she had tread,
After her journey she set them ablaze;
Once upon a Valentine when they met.

Listened to his heart more, rather than head,
Can't blame though; he was in a pubertal haze
When his heart for sorrow was not set.

I was aware of what held for him, his fate;
What didn't die was a heart full of craze.
Once upon a Valentine when they met
When his heart for sorrow was not set.

DEEPANJAN CHHETRI

Deepanjan Chhetri is an undergraduate studying at University of Calcutta.

20. GHOSTING

barely in the present
i'm the ghost of my own past
and a future that may never come

a small collection of stardust
fused to flesh moving through
time's pale illusion on automatic pilot
still praying for a miracle

somewhere deep inside
a small flame burns with a passion
no tears can drown

i rise each day floating on the hope
fueled by that flame
stubborn heart beating the waltz of life
in three-quarter time

RC DEWINTER

RC deWinter writes in several genres with a focus on poetry. She is also a digital artist and sometimes chanteuse. Her poetry is widely anthologized, notably in New York City Haiku (NY Times, February 2017), Nature In The Now (Tiny Seed Press, August 2019), Coffin Bell Two (March 2020), 2020 Summer Anthology: a Headrest for Your Soul (Otherworldly Women Press, July 2020), in print: 2River, Event, Genre Urban Arts, Gravitas, Meat For Tea: The Valley Review, the minnesota review, Night Picnic Journal, Prairie Schooner, Southword, among others and appears in numerous online literary journals.

21. DISSAPOINTMENT RUNS IN THE FAMILY

It's easy to fault the monoliths of salt for their sins,
as the doe-eyed chosen of creation
stumbling blindly towards its own tanglewire.
I do not care to share the number of nights
I have spent looking for your demise
at the bottom of a bottle,
nor do I dare to let the vapors of your name
dance upon my tongue.
Now that I have molted my own gooseflesh,
known the timbre of my own trees fall,
and enjoyed the comforting clutches of the familial bear trap,
I see the inky blackness from which you tried to reach me.
Life is a twisting labyrinth of the damned raising the damned
and you were once the spirited comet's tail,
all potential screeching across the night's sky,
before dissipating into nothingness.
These days your altar has crumbled into the unrecognizable
And I am left to worship the blood-rusted barbs within my own skin

STEVEN KEENE

Steven Keene is a 29-year-old Business Analyst from Southern Maine. When not working or writing, he can be found playing fetch with his cat Cricket. His work is inspired by strongly brewed coffee, politics, and frequent visits to open water.

22. AGAIN AND AGAIN

I am going off tomorrow
To a place, I never imagined I did go again
To a game of love
A place which I left with my Independence

I think I am drunk again
Drunk in this smell of yours again
The eyes and this feel
To the touch of our skins

Maybe this is no go again
Just like our pasts
We are burning indulging old flames
Soon we would drift apart

It's now been quite a while
My sheet still gives off your scent
My room still full of your things
Why we are with each other again and again? Yet being distant.

ISHAN MUKHOPADHYA

Ishan Mukhopadhya born and brought up in India. He wanted to narrate stories as forever as he can remember. Finally took the plunge to write his first story at the age of 14 after reading a book name of which he can't remember soon reading became his hobby and the way he would spend his free time most of the day. His first work may never see the light of the day but at the age of 17, he started posting his works on various Anonymous online forums and after years he started submitting his works to various competitions and publishers. One lone night in the fall of 2020 he sat at his desk and wrote a poem which became "Again and Again" and became his first work to be published. PS: He is just a cat disguised as a human who loves to write.

23. SECOND PERSON SINGULAR

If you should ever come upon this book
and open it and read between the lines
like damascene details on valentines
from back when they were cloth, and stop to look
awhile and wonder, you should not conclude
the you involved is you or anyone
particular. For it is everyone
and no one. Otherwise I would be sued.

Anonymous is a device to let
me unleash unabashed, sordid truth
with as much abandon as a hapless youth
running into the margins with half the words misspelt!
The fact I have not met you, as of yet,
does not mean what I've said has not been felt.

JAMES B. NICOLA

James B. Nicola is the author of five collections of poetry: Manhattan Plaza (2014), Stage to Page: Poems from the Theater (2016), Wind in the Cave (2017), Out of Nothing: Poems of Art and Artists (2018), and Quickening: Poems from Before and Beyond (2019). His decades of working in the theater as a stage director, composer, lyricist, playwright, and acting teacher culminated in the nonfiction book Playing the Audience: The Practical Guide to Live Performance, which won a Choice award. A Yale grad, he hosts the Hell's Kitchen International Writers' Roundtable at his library branch in Manhattan: walk-ins welcome.

24. LIGHT

A red glow peeks through my door every night,
It brushes the dark walls and leaves a rainbow of shadows,
and it sees apathetic nodding but it doesn't join my loner's dance,
and it hears eccentric melodies but it won't sing karaoke with me.

It oms
It projects
It emanates.

A white light announces its way every morning,
It bounces through green glass and off the arms of leafy tobacco paper,
and it livens the room with all of its rays,
and it moves along the plane of my face.

It expands
It radiates
It is above me.

XAVIER REYNA

Poet from the Rio Grande Valley.

25. OBSESSION

That dark grey cloud swirls in the horizon
It twists and moves of its own accord
A flash of light stares down while the large 'boom!!' mocks
Seek shelter to find there is none
Batter between the walls of glass as the clouds unfold around
The 'booms!!' turn into voices
The voices drive the storm
Growing smaller by the minute
Futile attempts to block out the sounds
The voices grow louder and imprint their bruises onto the soul
Protective layer of skin is washed away
The cold rattles the bones
Screaming a plea for respite
No one can stop the descent into madness
Anything left now is deteriorated into ash
The lone remaining voice blows what's left away

LINDSEY WENTZEL

Lindsey Wentzel/Muse Mesperyian was born in Plano, TX and grew up in Austin, TX. After high school, she attended the University of North Texas in Denton. After two years in college, she dropped out to travel the country by hitchhiking and riding freight trains. Panhandling for money and utilizing social services available for travelers. After many years of drug addiction, she sought help and eventually became sober and a productive member of society...most of the time.

26. WHERE STARS GO WHEN THEY DIE

Nothing lasts forever, not even the ones
made in heaven. And no, they don't simply
crash on the gloaming horizon

in sad solace. When they burn out like
embers, stars become immense in their
unbecoming. Enough to swallow up

everything in their paths. Everything. Ever
so dense, they slowly fade into oblivion.
Yet others die suddenly, in a silence

so vast only the universe can bear. They
try to stay alive by rekindling at first. But
it's only a matter of time before they

succumb to fate. All that remains is a
black hole, sucking life into a futility of the
forlorn. No escape from this relentless force.

When it's mourning, a dying star drowns
out the rest of the galaxy in quietude.

The stellar debris strewn across will form
new stars, sparking unexplored possibilities.

Remnants of you and me, colliding into
another we after us.

MELVIN TAN

Years ago, I asked myself: "If I die in my sleep, what is the one thing that I want my friends to remember?" Poetry, I decided. I never looked back.

27. CYCLE

It is the fatter end of the winter months.

the frog mother carries her children in a wicker basket

oil slick legs held together with slender ribbon

set in a cradle beside the brittle bouquet propped atop her sickly wife's bedside table

amongst the old painted pill box, glass of water which makes the cradle twitch.

the wife's expiration date reads *before spring* in a well-paced print

their frog children are almost too young to miss her.

It is buxom springtime.

by now these frog children have grown heads, faces

sing and dance about the ribbons, drape them like scarves

swing from them in tender zest, use them to suspend their carnival smiles

to cover the eyes of their dead mothers. Too slender for cerecloth

too sublime to hold a cure for whatever the wives had fallen to

these little frog children, their little wet hands

are older now, and wiser, can tie knots and go places

but still come home each springtime and weep for their mothers,

a thousand solemn croaks in perfect solitude.

later,

Humble autumn comes and goes

Bleak summer like a swathe of termites munching through sweet frog skin

they have reared children, sprouted moss across deckled backs

died, once, twice, gravesites packed under feet of siblings, brothers, children

twin mothers bathe them in salts, scrub the algae from their slender bones,

wring out the ribbons, nuclear gold beneath dirt plaque

lovely bones clink, again a bouquet

and the wives again waltz to their rhythm

AMELIA REED

My name is Amelia Reed, and I am hoping to submit my poem "Cycle" at 250 words for publication. The poem is intended to be a gentle yet mournful piece showing my connection to nature and to the seasons as a practicing Pagan. It is meant to help readers understand the peacefulness and purity of small things; small joys, such as baking pies with a loved one, are the same, in the end, as large joys, such as being accepted into the college of your choice. I, as a woman born and raised in San Francisco, don't see too much of seasonal variety myself. However, this poem marks my love for nature, even if that nature includes three seasons of winter and one of muggy summertime heat.-Amelia

28. THE ILLUSION

There's a difference
between the smoke and the cigarette,
what didn't happen,
what did,
and the fantasy of the id.

Hindsight is 20/20
where the wisdom is plentiful,
like a green hillside.
But the ego cannot follow
anything deep enough to be hollow.

I'm grateful for the dead illusion.
I mourned when it died,
but glad to wrap up the long road
that led me nowhere
but back to the first square.

AMANDA TUMMINARO

Amanda Tumminaro lives in the U.S. with her loving family and her cat. She's been published in The Scriblerus, The Nonconformist Magazine, and Grand Little Things, among others. Her chapbook, "The Flying Onion" (2018), was published by The Paragon Press.

29. TOO BUSY FOR TEARS

Our cliché for the divorcée, widow
and spinster is solitary sadness.
Self-pity is a tar pit that can lure
then envelop the many, the needy.

A rejected woman alone, collapsed
over her dinette table. Her sniffles
turn into sobs and then into long moans.
I do not know that pathetic woman.

Rather, I know her only in movies,
novels and the newspaper comic strips.
In *our* apartment, it was *le sang froid*.
Our single head of house had things to do.

My post-War parents, witty and pretty
wed in duty and lust, then really met.
Two toddlers later they learned that good looks
could not guarantee a long life of love.

Our mother did all for job and children,
without anger, minus spite and slander.
Late in life, she said she was too busy,
adding "I would not take the time to cry.

MICHAEL BALL

Michael Ball scrambled from newspapers through business and technical pubs. Born in OK
and raised in rural WV, he became more citified in Manhattan and Boston. One of the Hyde
Park Poets, he has moderate success placing poems including in Griffel, Gateway Review,
Havik Anthology, SPLASH!, Peregrine Journal, In Parentheses, and Reality Break Press.

30. MELANCHOLY MAN

Pensive sadness guards his heart
He lumbers his sorrow, his back broken
His hand's wilt, idle, lifeless
The absence of a lovers palm
He is more aware of that than not
Remorse has become his companion
He lost out
Gambled away his love
His prize?
A cash-out of loneliness
He lives his days in perceived isolation
Fearful to think
How he doesn't realise it yet.

SAMUEL PATRICK AVA ROBERTSON

My name is Samuel Patrick Ava Robertson I am a trans-man, from Scotland who is heavily present in the LGBT, English Literature and Art community, whilst also being a writer & poet writing about emotional subject matter as a means of self-expression. My main themes for my poems are the basis of folklore and nature

31. MY BODY IS A FRUIT SALAD AND YOU ARE A FORK

My body is a fruit salad, the
bladder an overripe pear
I tie myself off to stop the
juice from spilling down the
entirety of my over-washed denim.

My bowl is full of what you need.

I wash my papaya clean with
what is already inside of me
the fruit is clean if you want it to be
I say as I lay there, dried up.

Eat off me if you dare, I say to
you as you chew on the cracked raw
skin, and you are a fork, shiny silver
salivated by the spit of the other women
you have dipped your prongs into.

ELIZABETH GRACE WILLIAMS

Elizabeth Grace Williams currently resides in central Nebraska and is pursuing her Bachelor of Arts in English at the University of Nebraska at Kearney. Along with poetry, she also enjoys writing creative non-fiction and fiction. She received the Outstanding Poetry Award at the Student Language and Literature Conference and her work has appeared in The Carillon.

32. CALCULUS

We solved the differential of our existence by counting small stones;
but they said the depths of our minds were way too shallow.
Their analyst said we needed precise axioms
to capture the ghosts of departed quantities,
so they plotted our lives on their X-Y charts.
Their palmist read geometric woes
from the lines of our palms
and said: *"This is the limit to which your fish brains can function."*

But I ask, who gave them rights to run evaluation
and pose theorems of existence?
Who gave them the impetus to set standards of living?
Who said we are but indefinite integrals
and who made them higher order derivatives?

Oh, tell them! Tell them we know we know there is a rate of change,
we know the vicious circle is bound in continuity.
Tell them we don't need their almighty formula to solve the equation of our utter
confusion, we can fix our stochastic systems & can find the roots of our own identity.

Yes tell them! Tell them we shall cover the erotic distance
between dreams and reality, when speed and time share
a sweet romance.

SOONEST NATHANIEL

Soonest Nathaniel is a Poet and spoken word artist. He is the author of "Teaching My Father How To Impregnate Women," selected as winner of the 2017 RL Poetry Award. He was poet Laureate for 2014 Korea Nigeria Poetry Festival. His poems appear or are forthcoming in Rattle, Silver Blade, The Pedestal Magazine, FIYAH, Silver Blade Poetry, Northridge Review, Praxis Mag, Raven Chronicles, Wiki Column, Saraba, Loudthotz, Northridge Review, Reverbnation, Elsewhere, Scintilla, Erbacce UK, Kalahari Review, Sentinel Nigeria, and Many more.

33. RESOLVED

Each night with sad resolve I pray,
and long for your embrace.
But harsh the road,
and full of bumps,
the path, our tale, this race.

And though the howl of past defeat
be fixed within my ear.
I'll hold you close
with all my might
'till you can join me here.

STEPH THOMPSON

Steph Thompson is an American novelist and poet living outside Washington D.C. She is a graduate of UMCP and a CPA (Inactive) in the state of Maryland. When not writing, working, or wrangling four little ones, she can be found running local trails or reading in a cozy wingback at her favorite café (in a mask of course).

34. SHAMELESS

Clandestine
Sublime
Hidden gem
No need to hide
No need for fear
No need for regret
Forget regret
Live shamelessly
For with age comes wisdom
As youthful naiveté
Gives way
To maturity
Until the final moment
When one transcends
Towards eternity
Fearlessly

ALEX ANDY PHUONG

Alex Andy Phuong earned his Bachelor of Arts in English from California State University—Los Angeles in 2015. He was a former Statement Magazine editor who currently writes passionately. He has written film reviews for MovieBoozer, and has contributed to Mindfray. He writes hoping to inspire the ones who dream.

35. PINK BOYS AND BLUE GIRLS

Now, don't get me wrong
I crave to belong
I dream of the day when I finally become
A pretty pink girl or a perfect blue boy
Who lives by the sea
With love and faith and no jealousy
And has a cat named snuggles and no other troubles
But no matter how hard I travel the path
That may lead me to this life
My essence is golden,
Not rose or cerulean
And so I'm inclined to enter the aisle
Where every misshapen transforms
The unavoidable tragic
Into some kind of magic
This is a calling for every lost soul
Who wanders around craving to belong
I ask you to join me in this new travesty
Where we will find an empty forest
And live in wondrous harmony

SOFIA LEVIAGUIRRE

Passionate about the magical transformation of language.

36. BUNCH

My cat sleeps on his side,
Spilt legs bunched,
As if wrapped
With a rubber band—
A puffing
White rose
Bouquet

My cat dreams on his side
Of being arced
Across a dance floor
To a glittery forest
Of clammy arms

My cat awakes on his back
While I was counting
His fishbone ribs
With my nose,
Then flops onto his side
To count my nose
With his nose.

RICH GLINNEN

Best of the Net nominee, Rich Glinnen, enjoys bowling, and eating gruyere with his cats at his home in Bayside, NY. His work can be read in Kenneth Warren's Lakewood House Organ, at foliateoak.com, petrichormag.com, underwoodpress.com/ruescribe, Tumblr, and Instagram. His wife calls him Ho-ho.

37. KNOWLEDGE IS BEAUTIFUL

If she were a princess, I'd court her.
But never to join her in holy matrimony be able to would I,
For to no one does she belong in full ownership.
She never wears the same gown twice
And even if perchance your eyes lay on a familiar sewn detail,
It'd look different to another pair,
Like what was that knick-knack, was it blue and black or white and gold?
Interpretations vary…
Beauty is in the eye of the beholder, after all…?

NADIA BENJELLOUN

Nadia Benjelloun is from Tangier, Morocco. She graduated from the American School of Tangier in 2017. As well as freelance writer, she is also an associate editor for Typehouse Literary Magazine. She has been featured in The Literary Yard, Eskimo Pie, In Parenthesis Journal, The Scarlet Leaf Review, DM du Jour at Danse Macabre, The Book Smuggler's Den, The Sagebrush Review, The Abstract Elephant and many more.

38. THE CARPENTERS

I harvest fine-coarse wood from fallen trees
lying in the forest of my heart-mind,
evergreen softwood that bends in the breeze
and leafy hardwood that is disinclined,
Hard-soft wood to frame the jigsawing words,
a nest for metaphor to say it slant,
grain running straight as gregarious shorebirds,
and spruced words filed and arrayed to enchant.
You too are a member of the guild,
a heart bending in giddy confusion,
puzzling over mind-images to build
a new forest of our profusion.
We are the tongue and groove of poetry,
but you are the last nail that sets words free.

ERIC BRODY

I began writing poetry seriously last year. I find it a necessary comfort in the age of COVID. My goal is to use strong imagery and suggestive word choice to convey an idea that is not obvious nor obscure. This is my delicate balance.-Eric

39. ESCAPE

One word
Six letters
Used against me
to make me feel so guilty
       for this desire
        that burns my soul
        like fire
Any dream that involves leaving
is now pronounced
/rəniːŋ əweɪ /
Tricked me into thinking
I had to stay
& FACE. IT.
Face it?
More like fuck this.

But these six letters
[Will forever be etched]
in the bark of my tree
like the initials of two lovers.
ESCAPE

ADRIENNE WITEK

Adrienne Witek is a Chicago born aspiring writer and student of life. She studied Spanish as an undergrad and is particularly intrigued by the intricacies of language. In her spare time Adrienne can be found convincing friends and acquaintances alike not to give up on love for the world.

40. SOLUS

We sometimes forget
when to release our hands from the throttle
u-shaped roads, chiseled cinderblocks, and
industrial volumes of perspiration percolate
from necklines forming a crevice
on tanned skin. we pretermit ourselves
from being free from relentless obligation.

This consternation of inner voices--
the control freaks, the dictators, the autocrats
dominating our minds, preventing us from
letting go when it's what we need the most
And instead of our hearts, our heads
act the provost. Incessant exertion doesn't
enlighten us-- it only deprives our toil of
foresight.
So let go of this Orwellian nightmare.

I release our hands from the steering
in hopes of one day seeing
the orchestra of cooperated vigor,
hearing the basses and french horns
and wondering-- was my solo ever
as good? and just like that, one by one,
we throw a coup d'etat on the depraved
faculties of ourselves that are telling us to
go it alone.

And just like that, the engine revs, and
we are sitting in the backseat knowing
of preeminence due to alliance;
and coalition; and synergy; and all of the
foremost limbs that we
rely on.

TARUNI TANGIRALA

Taruni is a writer from Texas whose work appears in Réapparition Journal and others. Her work hopes to capture the essence of humanism and emotion in order to combat divisiveness that constantly plagues our society.

41. LIKE I BURDENED YOU

the soft needled pines,
and tall maples and oaks
brought me peace;
the babbling brooks and laughing creeks
insisted better days would arrive—
was a comfort to find a hiding place where
your wounding words could not
find me,
a place that gave me distance
from you was my heaven on earth;
you always rubbed it in my face that you
adopted me like i owed you everything
for all the hate and rage you gave me
instead of love—
you wanted me to respect you,
but you didn't give me any;
treated me like your personal punching bag
and i was never allowed to talk to anyone about
our fights because i wasn't allowed to burden
anyone with my existence, i guess, like i burdened you.

LINDA M. CRATE

Linda M. Crate's (she/her) works have been published in numerous magazines and
anthologies both online and in print. She is the author of six poetry chapbooks, the latest of
which is: More Than Bone Music (Clare Songbirds Publishing House, March 2019). She's
also the author of the novel Phoenix Tears (Czykmate Books, June 2018). Recently she has
published two full-length poetry collections Vampire Daughter (Dark Gatekeeper Gaming,
February 2020) and The Sweetest Blood (Cyberwit, February 2020).

42. SPOILED CLUTCHES

I'm a prisoner in flesh bound chains
A being with disease in my veins
The defunct plan of a greater cause
That big bang theory of universal gauze
      I'm an ape that learned too damn much
A creature with the gold Midas touch
The pendulum in a pit of genetic code
That cookie cut pattern, which glowed
      I'm a short-lived miracle of clay and straw
A masticating mouth with hinged drop jaw
The problem with all that's wrong in the land
That pinprick of hope for something so grand
      I'm an echo of some schmuck named Adam
A monster created from an ocean of bedlam
The star in a ten trillion cast epic saga
That little bit part in a microcosmic drama
      I'm the one who broke the magnanimous mold
A treasure dug up from a long-lost world of old
The heart of the plot of the greatest mystery ever
That enigma which will question for now and forever
      I'm a demigod tied to a screen die cast in silver
A spoon on the platter that serves only fine liver
The drunkard of life and all that it has to offer
That large cache of riches in an Earthly coffer
      I'm the warm corpse that doesn't know any better
A dream from a god that's only getting wetter
The ember in a fire that's flared out of control
That speck of light in the deepest darkest hole
      I'm the link in a chain that will eventually break
A condemned waif who was displayed upon the stake
The astute judge that's gaffed every single case
That lost, frightened calf in the deadliest race
      I'm creator of too many things to put on a list
A destroyer of all that is so desperately missed
The corrupted king that's ruled far too long
That sheep in the flock from that childhood song

I'm the story that's been lost through translation
A brother and sister to every creature in creation
The good or the evil depending on the situation
That right for the wrong when wrong is salvation
I'm nothing more than a warm-blooded body
A whale of a mind that forgot it was shoddy
The quirk in a world full of steadfast laws
I'm the beast on Earth that's born out of flaws

DAVID GRUBB

David Grubb, a retired Coastguard Warrant Officer, has creatively written since childhood, yet career/family always came first. He's changing that aspect of life and loving every minute. His work appears in Touchstone, Toasted Cheese, 1:1000, Sixfold.org, The Elevation Review, Every Day Fiction, The Abstract Elephant, The Bookends Review, and Wingless Dreamer's Heartfelt Poetry Collection.

43. MESMERIZED

He looked up as I walked in.
His tight blue jeans hugging his long legs,oh so thin.
Eyes of gray.
What the hell was I going to say?
Tattoos of vibrant colors sleeved on his right arm.
Smiling showing his perfect white teeth was he full of charm?
We haven't said hello out loud.
How he stood out in the crowd.
Body language saying it all.
Looking at him as I tried not to fall.
As he made his way over to me, butterflies in my stomach
and light on my feet.
He sat next to me grabbing his seat.
I looked up at him and said we finally meet.
He raised an eyebrow and said sweet.
He put his arm around my thin frame.
Ever since I haven't been the same.

KIM LISTRO

My name is Kim. I live in CT. I'm 48. At the age of 12. I started writing song lyrics. I'll never forget the first one. I showed my grandfather. He was so proud. Everyone knew. So exciting. At twelve I also started writing short stories. A great way to escape. Along with reading every book I could get my hands on. (I still read like that today.) When I turned nineteen my other grandfather surprised me with a used typewriter. It meant so much to me. I typed away my stories.At nineteen I also fell into poetry. I hope you enjoy the lighter side of my poem. I have many sides. Thank you to my grandparents for believing in me.

44. THE FAWN

The bride lowers the veil of lace.
A subtle smile beams the moonglow.
The clouds weep.
 Through the shroud, a sinister rustle.
A pair of eyes.
An abyss.
Bliss.
The fawn gracefully bounds.
A pause. The pierce of pensive eyes.
Once again it leaps, yearning.

KYLE SISITSKY

Kyle Sisitsky is a student who thoroughly enjoys all kinds of poetry. Residing in New York, he began writing at the young age of six. His favorite poems are those written in the rhythmic iambic pentameter.

45. LADDER TO THE MOON

Over mountains soaked in malachite,
under the pill-cutter-sliced moon,
turquoise sky, I'm standing
on nothing, going nowhere,
body an anvil suit
tethered to snapping scorpions, quicksand
pools, glittering mirages
that have eroded me
stone to sand, along paths of boulders,
rabbit holes breaking bones
into dust.

Between flurry and grace
jasmine's siren
invites me to leap
star to star, across milky streams
and cobalt seas
where I can evanesce
into the lunar light.

(This is an ekphrastic poem based on Georgia O'Keeffe's painting
"Ladder to the Moon")

JUDY TAYLOR

Judy Taylor is a nonfiction author and poet. She has published two books, *Dharma Cats* and *Living Lightly with Lyme*. Some of her essays and poems have appeared in recent print and online publications. Judy enjoys life in the San Francisco Bay Area writing, making art, and playing with her cat. Through her poetry, she attempts to reveal the tender heart of humanity and her hope for a better world.
Hope that works for you.

46. HIDING PLACE, TABLE FOR ONE

Plains in Africa have no sight to gawk,
nor mouths for tattling.
Rainless, dessert clouds neither possess memory,
nor recall Chile's line of mountains.

God cast His planet abroad archipelagos ,
and peninsulas ,
and deltas ,
and seas .

He created a fathomless bowl of possible possibilities ,
yet in a moment they condensed.
Unknown voids were revealed amidst particles.
An existence fatally cooled after it's heated expansion.

A solitary droplet remained, racing for the cliff's edge of a jaw;
thoughts are foes to the wise just as they be to fools.
Once the present is past, time has no choice but to decay the facts,
and guilt requires no name for a reservation.

If Michigan's blizzard has no acquaintance with India's typhoon,
then let their indifference to carnage be a shelter to me,
a wayward creation,
famished for peace.

KELLY HESTER

Born and raised in Texas, Kelly Hester has room in her heart for both the conveniences of city life and the wide expanse of the country. She is currently a licensed Physical Therapist Assistant, but has co-authored and self-published three novel with her parents in the past. As a follower of God and Jesus, she is thankful for every day she is given and wishes to learn as much as possible about our Creator. God's influence on Kelly has brightened her life and His gift of authorship to her has been a blessing she could never thank Him enough for."

47. MARIANA

What laws of life determine the value
Of pain, of loss, of dreams and desire?
What does one think, say or do
To dry the tears, to kindle the fire?

There is no rationalization,
For the heart knows not.
There is no subjugation
For what passion has wrought.

Lips quiver and long to be kissed;
A wound that hurts but does not bleed.
A heart of devotion is cruelly dismissed;
The love it knew was merely perceived.

How to explain why this heart aches,
Why the tears fall, why the soul is sad.
Perhaps one day soon it'll know what it takes
To rejoice—not weep—for what it never had.

VANESSA MARIE CARON

VanessaMarieCaron is a young stay-at-home-mother of four and a passionate individual, consistently striving to emulate emotionally character-led novels, poems and short stories alike. Her style uses imagery with a poetic undercurrent. Writing is her art of choice, a tool for expression, a way by which she transcends to higher places. Writing novels is her main love however, she endeavours to refine her craft and uncover her stylistic preferences through literary journals and poetry. When not writing, Vanessa bounces between being a contemplative in nature, an eccentric fitness junkie and an avid horse lover.

48. BULLETPROOF HEART

The concept of love is an interesting thing
One day you shall love them, the next day they leave.
You take a big piece of your fragile heart, and share it,
Hoping you won't fall apart.

You hand them the gun filled with bullets inside,
Sharing your secrets, ignoring the pride.
You trust them your body, you trust them your soul,
You trust them your love- the treasure of all.

You hope that the trigger is not being pulled,
Yet you become blinded and end up being lured.
You tend to come off as a bulletproof shield,
Yet we often tend to get lost on the battle field.

The battle of love, the battle of hope,
The two souls connecting and tightening the rope .
You hope when you fall, they would catch you still,
They will push you back and help when your ill.

The ones who have truly good intentions and care,
Tend to be treated quite unfair.
It's very unfortunate that those with big hearts,
Are often mistreated and played just like darts.

It's very important to always stay clean,
To have good intentions, since big hearts do win.
To never give up when you are being hurt,
To always keep going and loving a lot.

By loving a lot I don't mean you love others
And give them the love that they don't tend to see.
I mean love yourself, it should be unconditional,
Only then your mind will be set of to being free .

You shall care for you, to appreciate you,
To value yourself and be your own crew.
Acknowledge your worth and never give up,
Regardless what life has been putting you through, fill your own cup.

You are so unique, there is no one like you,
Express it, allow it to shine through you.
Value your mind and value your body,
You won't get another like anybody

Value your soul and treasure your heart,
And never allow yourself to fall apart.

DALIAL MUTALLAPOVA

Dalial Mutallapova is an aspiring young poet born in Russia, studying in the UK. Writing poems allows her to express her emotions freely and overcome any obstacles in life by allowing the words to flow on paper. She wants to change the world for the better by helping individuals become happier. Dalial is 17 years old and loves to travel and explore new opportunities. A note from author "don't be afraid to accept yourself, the world needs more people like you".

49. FACE

Like the ocean tide travel wave
        It is written on the distinction of her face
drowning in the emotional weight
        passing up and down along the pace
fighting through the heavily thunderstorm way
        In a tirelessly effort display
With a much courageous and praise
        In an unwaveringly stay
Of a mother own instinct pray
        To protect her child as always
with her unselfishness portray
        to provide for a better way
in seeking for her child's needs
        Even mean putting herself at last
Only we all know how much of
        a mother's love is so precious
with her sacrifice that has been made
        That is incomparable like no other jewelry
    can showcase
Not even money can buy and trade
        This is the reason why we must never betray
her
        To see all the above that stand
A gracious smile on her look

HANH CHAU

Hanh resides from San Jose, California USA. During her spare time, she enjoys writing, listening to music, spending time with family and etc. She works for Kaiser Hospital as Patient Services Representative for 16 years. She has a bachelor's degree in business administration and an MBA.

50. MIRRORED SALTS

Oleander fields of crystallin waves rolling under.
Gently to soften its feet
sulked in morning dipped in its edge
braised a new transparency

the salts enrichments
like capers and fine wines.

Lemon grass votives like star dust.
Peach sorbets, and chamomile whispers,
pink roses and purple violets.

Light brightens the dusted room,
and lifts like a veil hidden behind clouds,
to be seen like tranquility awakens.

The aromas scented potpourris embellished,
eucalyptus, lavender, jasmine and sage,
cinnamon, and ginger infusions an ambiance,
flames romanced on candle wicks.

All things come as all things go,
we must be faced with oppression
to see the things which lye asunder secret surfaces.

EVE CHILICAS

Eve Chilicas is a writer and poet, who has published poetry In literary journals and chapbooks, she is a member of Poetry Society of America, and continues to creatively write and aspire the endeavors of her passion.

52. MEMOIR OF A SHADE

I saw her in Troy once. Or maybe it was her other.
Peeling off the hanging skin, loose on every inch;
Ripped flesh, raw; rusty stitches feeding on ancient blood:
an open wound that drips tears
in the barren fountain of the forgotten.
Emptying her full mouth
from the words she never said; smothering the burden
Of her name.
Now she straightens the thread
to cut the last string of separation.

A farewell to her hollow past,
a tender kiss before the final turn:
And the shade – becomes her.

there you are, stapled to your martyrdom.
how did you end up here?

ELENA MOSCHOU

Elena Moschou was born in Greece in 1999. She graduated from the Hellenic American College in 2017 prior to being accepted into the Department of *English Language and Literature*, School of Philosophy, National Kapodistrian University of Athens. She is in her senior year of studies and her favorite courses include Creative Writing, Post-war British Drama, Restoration Comedy and Psycholinguistics. Ms Moschou is particularly interested in the works of Shakespeare. Upon completion of her current studies she plans to continue with a postgraduate degree abroad aspiring to pursue a career in academic research or the publishing industry. In her spare time, she enjoys studying Spanish and reading historical fiction and fantasy. Elena loves creating poems through experimentation with words and concepts. In 2016, she participated in Youth Summits of the UN, UNICEF, Red Cross and IOM in Switzerland, as a member of the *Women Rights and Diversity* Club of her school.

51. DEPARTURE

The lady in the old house;
All alone, cold and caved,
She couldn't do anything but browse,
And let the past memories be paved.

She once told all to leave,
For she was fed up with their growing demands.
But never she knew that she would grieve,
The departure of those who she commands.

Acts cannot be undone;
Past cannot be changed;
Little did she knew that she had all the doors to her satisfaction being shun,
Her happiness was far away, caged.

DEEPAKSHI SHARMA

An avid reader and poetry lover, Deepakshi Sharma is a student of Psychology. She is a keen observer and creative writer. Fond of singing and writing, she grew around learning the value of literature and culture. With ample support and guidance from her sister, she began writing poetry. Started off as a teenager trying to bind rhyming words together to form a poem, she has come a long way knowing how poetry is much more than just rhymes. She tries to pen down whatever she observes and feels; and gives it a unique blend of it's own. She aims at helping people realise how a simple piece of poetry can impact many lives positively; reiterating it's value as a mode of communication.

53. GROWING PAINS

Her life is like a chess set
It includes most who she's met
Each person is a piece
To her they were all beasts

She never look at the other side as foe
But how was she supposed to know
She had thought the others were loyal
It turns out they just made her blood boil

Aren't friends supposed to last forever?
Friend has the word end it in, how clever
Almost as if from the start
Things are supposed to fall apart

They took her army one by one
Until there were barely none
She felt alone because she was trapped
In a world she felt that humanity was lacked

Her king was exposed
She was clearly enclosed
Nowhere to hide
She was forced to abide

PHOEBE MILLER

Phoebe Miller is currently living in New York. She is studying biology with minors in chemistry and theology at St John's University. She loves to write and explore museums. Whenever the opportunity arises to do volunteer work she jumps in whether it is fundraising or working with children. In her free time, she loves hanging out with her friends and two wonderful cats.

54. REBORN AN ANGEL

The snow was falling down like confetti.
Her breathing was sparse, and her eyes were heavy.
Yet she was not afraid or unsteady.
She smiled and sighed like she was ready.
To die a girl and be reborn an angel...
She walks towards the divine light eternally faithful.
She bows her hand in prayer and is grateful,
To join her heavenly father in the clouds of the graceful.
She willingly trades her life for a pair of angel wings.
She will watch over her loved ones, she will belong to everything.
And in the misty morning light when the clouds gather for worshiping.
You can feel her warmth from the sun, you can hear the angels sing

AMANDA JANE

AmandaJane grew up on the maigical literature of Edgar Allen Poe, and the fantastical artwork of Tim Burton. As a kid, she would spend all day making up songs and nursery rhymes that are still dear to her heart today. They range from random adventures of talking soggy sandwiches, to magical unicorns without horns. Saving all of her stories and rereading them is a time capsule that takes her back to this young girl that saw the world with wacky characters, bright colours, and armed with her magic wand *(pencil),* could spread her magic. Keeping that little girl alive, she invites you to take an adventure alongside her imaginative words.

55. IN SIMPLE TERMS

He received his froyo with gummy bears,
A faraway innocence on his face
While Daddy snuck several nervous stares,
Hoping for an emotional safe space.

Attempting to explain in simple terms
The current domestic situation
Between spoonfuls of cream-coated sour worms
And stale euphemistic complications.

"Not getting along" was once a school phrase
Designated for petty playground fights;
Now 'twas the context behind which one stays
And which one visits on specified nights.

Though freedom from blame was often affirmed,
The eight-year-old still invisibly squirmed.

SAM HENDRIAN

Sam Hendrian is a poet and filmmaker living in Los Angeles but originally from the Chicago suburbs. He strives to foster a culture of empathy and sincerity through the art he creates.

56. INTER-GALACTIC BLISS

The moon and the stars are sending waves across the cosmos!
Their infinite union so sacred and yet so rare.
The fragments of time and space in a constant battle between art and fiction.
Dying to understand their milky existence.
A shimmering eclipse of endless wonder and illusion...
A constellation of fear and envy.
The bright and shining star and the luminous shadow hovering around it.
An inter-galactic romance blossoming from within,
Threatened by an inexplicable life force from another universe.
Sending waves across the galaxy and heatwaves to its earthly inhabitants.
A clouded optical illusion created by Zeus.
An electrifying sense of nostalgia, raining down on the hearts of every believer.
For the curious soul and the whimsical dreamer...
This is the beginning of a worm holed nightmare, spinning on the Earth's axis.

TOWERA GIFT MUGHOGHO

Towera Gift Mughogho is a creative writer. Born and raised in the warm heart of Africa, otherwise known as Malawi.Starting her writing from the tender age of 22, Towera forged her own path towards becoming a writer. Mastering the art of storytelling from many different perspectives, ranging from originality, whimsical humor and wordplay that keeps the reader guessing.She does this through a visual scope of metaphorical descriptions, designed to tap into the mind of the individual.Poking at what's left of their childlike imagination.She draws her inspiration from novels, movies, and short comic videos. The whole essence of poetry has always been an idea in the back of her mind, a skill that is constantly being crafted and moulded into better forms of writing.

57. EVERYTHING IS A GOD DAMNED SLAMMING DOOR

You and I depreciate like the saggy mottled couch
bought for our living room too many years ago.
Images blur as you stagger past my shadow.
You, my old man, slam and bang
around the kitchen like
a bull in a china closet.

Me, your once pristine lady, is a prisoner
of her high expectations-- each other's everything.
Love at first sight was so full,
its emptiness draining the last vestiges of caring.

"Can you hear yourself?"
your mouth curls,
your finger points--
piercing me inside

Our once parallel souls, *now*
like an old toy or the saggy mottled couch,
like my regret and your anger, reprised
as a goddamned slamming door.

CLEM VAHE

I'm a published writer--albeit an unpaid one. I use absurdist humor to depict the everyday
tribulations of humans in our society. - Clem

58. HUMIDITY

All caught up in the moment
You said what you felt
And I said what I thought
And the words hung
Heavy in the air
Echoing in the ensuing silence
Refusing to dissolve
A drippingly damp humidity
Not evaporating

And you stared at me
And I stared at you
Neither of us disbelieving
But both of us angry and hurt
Nonetheless
And you turned
And walked away
And I simply watched you go
Filled with worry and relief

ROSE MENYON HEFLIN

Rose Menyon Heflin is an emerging poet, artist, and photographer from Wisconsin who loves nature and travel. Her camera is named Nessie after the Loch Ness Monster, and her machete is named Carmen after the opera protagonist. Among other venues, her work has recently been published or is forthcoming in Ariel Chart, Asahi Haikuist Network, Bramble, The Closed Eye Open, The Daily Drunk, Dreich Magazine, Eastern Structures, The Ekphrastic Review, Haikuniverse, The Light Ekphrastic, Littoral Magazine, Please See Me, Plum Tree Tavern, Red Alder Review, Red Eft Review, Sparked Literary Magazine, Three Line Poetry, Trouvaille Review, Visual Verse, and The Writers Club. As an obsessive-compulsive, she strongly prefers hugging trees instead of people.

59. CRIMSON BROWN

I cannot brush it off.
It has stained the pale tint of my skin
my nose
my feet
some old linen
the shade of crimson brown.

I feel it sink deep under my skin
and poison my veins and blood.
I'm afraid that I will let it win
and take over me like a flood.

Soon I fear that all will gloat
and observe the day I drown.
They will watch my body drift afloat
in a sea of crimson brown.

SELAH ADERYN

Selah Aderyn, going by her pen name when writing for the public, is a young self-published poet. She lives in her home in Oregon studying backyard birds and making music along with writing poetry and prose. Follow her at @selah_aderyn_poetry to read more of her work and to be updated on her books

60. ME 2 YOU

Lust, The cardinal desire
sexy, hot and full of fire
I want to feel this with you

Envy, Is how I see the world
Longing, bitter, and resentful
I want to change, to be with you

Vaine, It's the end of me
arrogant, destructive, ego
I want to overcome with you

Regret, Is the core of my design
Sad, helpless and pittyful
I want to stop this, myself, once I'm with you

Hope, Is something I've never lost
my present, my future, my faith
I want to believe I'll be with you

But believing wont work,
I can not stop,
No one can overcome this,
But could you conqueour it?
This doubt that is absolute?

JUSTIN MCGEORGE

Justin McGeorge is a 26-year-old African-American male. Since he was little, he's been raised in a military family, being born In Oceanside, California, but having Jacksonville, North Carolina as his home for most of his life. Justin is currently slinging food at Logans Roadhouse, and when he's not at his job, he's writing poems, fixing computers, and hitting the gym. Alongside writing, music has also been a deep-seated passion for Justin throughout his life, being proficient in playing the trumpet, baritone, and Kalimba. He has studied for three years at Western Carolina University as an English Literature major and intends to finish his studies soon. Once his studies are complete, he would like to pursue a career in Social Services.

61. THE BIG BLUE SEA

Without truly feeling, I stared at the big blue sea.
Walking in a daze, I wondered how it all could be.

As the lights brightened, my self-awareness faded.
All and any past feelings of joy soon vacated.

Trembling, I felt trapped behind my own eyes.
Seeing an unclear hazy scene, I let free my cries.

Not believing the water was there, my feet felt the flood.
My tears slowly turned into falls of saturated blood.

Wisping away tears, feeling weak and done.
I held myself up and began to feel gone.

I walked towards and stared at the next wave
Not knowing what path to expect fate to pave

CLAIRE HOELSCHER

Claire Hoelscher lives in Texas. She grew up as a competitive gymnast and loved every part of it. When she was not in the gym, she enjoyed reading and traveling with her family. In high school she was required to write a poem for her English II class. Writing that poem led her to find the beauty in poetry and how much she enjoys writing it. Claire is currently a high school senior with plans to continue her education and obtain a degree in Child Development. In addition to her education, she works as a gymnastics coach and continues to write poetry in her spare time.

62. MOTHER TO SON

I see you lying in front of the fireplace from tiny boy to young man
a peace there
restless transitions made more content
a soul relieved to once again be comforted by the dancing flames
instead of terrified of them

I saw you retreat from the coals
smoke filling your sanctuary
grasping for ease

I saw you choking on fumes
an anger there
stubborn fists swiping at air

I see regret wedged in new lines on your forehead
a lingering sense of self-betrayal
but your lips curled in a soft smile
an awareness there
elation that the hearth remained lit during your absence

I see a tiny boy drawn into the light
your face leaning against the heat
brimming with wonder

I see a young man eagerly fanning the flames
embers winking in his brown eyes
a weight shed
wider shoulders better prepared to hold it

LUKE CARMOSINO

Luke Carmosino is a junior at the University of Wisconsin studying Economics and History. A voracious reader and autodidact since a young age, Luke pursues his passions with excitement and dedication. He first found inspiration in nature: a childhood spent tromping in the woods and exploring the wilds of natural places instilled in him a deep love for the outdoors and the beauty that came with it. The small boy who ran outside to play in every rainfall and spent his teen years running cross country throughout his native Hudson River Valley now considers writing not just one of his hobbies but also a budding profession. From poetry to prose to researched opinion, the craft of writing is a landscape he can't stop exploring.

63. THIS BODY ISN'T YOURS

For mama Segi's daughter
home was a place where

her body did not belong to her
the man *she* called father

had known the sacred room
of her over ripened body.

it started with sitting on his lap
telling her to move gently

home would have been where
her father's hand

won't fiddle with her *too* little moons
but home was her father praying between her legs.

she tried talking to her mother
but her tongue seared with silence and fear

her skin held all his ungodly prints
the night he came to her room to put her to sleep

he came on her night dress
her slender thighs

had become a ground for his libations
body reeked of sin and sweat.

she laid there in halves like bread broken for supper
hoping that death will snatch her lingering Soul

It did
with his sins streaking down

from her slit wrist
like rain running down a glass window

in thick red
home was now her body in a coffin.

he did not mold her
so she returned *it* back to her maker.

EMESOWUM CHIDOZIE

Emesowum Chidozie is an undergraduate student from the University of Nigeria, Nsukka. He is currently studying Mechanical Engineering but loves to indulge in creative writing(poetry) as a way to dissipate emotions rather than bottle them up. He usually goes by the pen name "Georgie". He looks up to writers like Charles Bukowski, Chris Abani and Romeo Oriogun to mention a few. He describes poetry as "oxygen for the soul"; even when he tries to leave poetry, poetry does not leave him

64. FIGHT NIGHT

Faster than a precipitous squall
The ivy spreads and scales the wall
Landlocking it's quarried structure suchlike Nepal
To conquer all collusive knees march with enthrall

Through the cracks wails the ominous battlefield call
Preambling the turnacets medics tightly tie to stall
Profanity ptyalises saturating crimson red gall
But with time all vitiated empires will fall

Slacked-jaws hang with fascination and appall
Congesting the receiving friend's line down the hall
Unable to order the perturbation from short to tall
All rubberneckers wear a one size fits all shawl

Barbwire installed to snag camouflaged words that crawl
Restricting insidiousness to minify the onslaught to befall
Just two will do for a high noon quick draw
Sometimes protecting the house is a merciless law

LINLEY MICHAEL CROCKER

Linley Michael Crocker was born, raised and currently resides in the small Southern town of Campobello, South Carolina. Art has always breathed inside of her, but poetry did not become the rise and fall of her chest until a year ago. In the rhythm of written words she found a way to turn her inside out and let her heart dry in the sun. By day she flips houses with her family and by night she writes.

" Believe in yourself "

"I want to use this opportunity to thank all the participants, Winglessdreamer's team and community members to make this publication possible. Thanks for the support and well-wishes."
–Ruchi Acharya (Wingless Dreamer Founder)

WRITE. FEEL. PUBLISH

If you liked our work, kindly do give us reviews on Amazon.com/winglessdreamer. It will mean a lot to our editorial team. You can also tag or follow us on:

Instagram: @winglessdreamer1 @ruchi_acharya

Facebook: www.facebook.com/winglessdreamer

Mail us: Editor: editor@winglessdreamer.com

Sales: sales@winglessdreamer.com

Website: www.winglessdreamer.com

You can also support our small creative community through donation: www.paypal.me/winglessdreamer

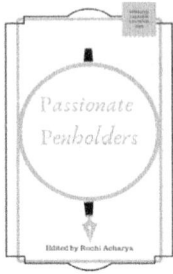

Passionate Penholders   Passionate Penholders II   Art from heart

Daffodils   Father and I   Sunkissed

Tunnel of lost stories   Overcoming Fear   The Rewritten

Fruits of our Quarantine

Magic of motivational

Diversity

Dark poetry collection

A glass of wine with Edgar

Made in the USA
Middletown, DE
08 March 2021